CPS-Morrill School Library

34880 00010631 5

Richardson, Adele   598.9 RIC
Eagles : birds of prey

W9-ASR-774

DATE DUE

598.9
RIC

Richardson, Adele
Eagles : birds of prey

Morrill School Library
Chicago Public Schools
6011 S. Rockwell
Chicago, IL 60629

The Wild World of Animals

Eagles

Birds of Prey

by Adele D. Richardson

Consultant:
Joseph L. Shelnutt
Director
Southeastern Raptor Rehabilitation Center
Auburn University, Alabama

Bridgestone Books
an imprint of Capstone Press
Mankato, Minnesota

C1   2003   13.95

Bridgestone Books are published by Capstone Press
151 Good Counsel Drive, P.O. Box 669, Mankato, Minnesota 56002
http://www.capstone-press.com

Copyright © 2002 Capstone Press. All rights reserved.
No part of this book may be reproduced without written permission from the publisher.
The publisher takes no responsibility for the use of any of the materials
or methods described in this book, nor for the products thereof.
Printed in the United States of America.

Library of Congress Cataloging-in-Publication Data
Richardson, Adele, 1966–
    Eagles: birds of prey/by Adele D. Richardson.
    p. cm.—(The wild world of animals)
    Includes bibliographical references (p.24) and index.
    Summary: A brief introduction to eagles, describing their physical characteristics, habitat,
    young, food, predators, and relationship to people.
    ISBN 0-7368-1136-2
    1. Eagles—Juvenile literature. [1. Eagles.] I. Title. II. Series.
QL696.F32 R5354 2002
598.9'42—dc21   2001003944

Editorial Credits
Erika Mikkelson, editor; Karen Risch, product planning editor; Linda Clavel, illustrator
    and designer; Heidi Schoof, photo researcher

Photo Credits
Corel/Predators, 1
Dave Watts/TOM STACK & ASSOCIATES, 10
Erwin and Peggy Bauer/TOM STACK & ASSOCIATES, 8
International Stock LLC/Ronn Maratea, 20
McDonald Wildlife Photography, 4, 6
PhotoDisc, Inc. (texture), 2, 3, 6, 10, 12, 18, 22, 23, 24
Robert McCaw, 18
Robin Brandt, cover
Thomas Kitchin/TOM STACK & ASSOCIATES, 12
Tom and Pat Leeson, 16
Visuals Unlimited/David H. Ellis, 14

1 2 3 4 5 6 07 06 05 04 03 02

Table of Contents

bald eagle

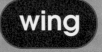

wing

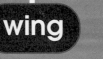

wing

beak

talons

Eagles

Eagles are large birds. Eagles have a curved beak and strong talons. Black or dark brown feathers cover most eagles' bodies. Some eagles have white or golden feathers on their heads and shoulders. Eagles weigh between 4.5 and 15 pounds (2 and 6.8 kilograms).

talon

a sharp claw

FUN FACTS

Eagles have eyesight that is four times better than a human's. An eagle can see other animals as far away as 1 mile (1.6 kilometers).

bald eagle

Eagles Are Birds of Prey

Eagles are birds of prey. They hunt and eat other animals. Birds of prey use their strong beaks to tear meat. They have powerful wings and hollow bones. These features help birds of prey fly. Birds of prey also have good eyesight.

hollow

having empty space inside it

harpy eagle

An Eagle's Habitat

An eagle's habitat is where it lives. Eagles are found all around the world except Antarctica. Harpy eagles live in rain forests. Bald eagles build their nests in trees near water. Some eagles live in jungles, forests, or deserts.

rain forest
a forest of tall trees that grows where it is warm and rainy all year

FUN FACTS

The white bellied
sea eagle eats fish
and sea snakes.

white bellied sea eagle

What Do Eagles Eat?

Eagles eat small animals. Bald eagles eat mostly fish. Bumps on eagles' feet help them hold onto slippery fish. Golden eagles eat rabbits, ground squirrels, and other birds. They use their strong talons to grasp prey.

grasp
to grab onto
something tightly

bald eagles

FUN FACTS

The bald eagle is not bald. It has white feathers on its head. Bald eagles have nearly 7,000 feathers on their bodies.

Mating and Hatching

Eagles build a large nest before mating. They mate in early spring. Bald eagles in Florida sometimes mate in winter. The female eagle lays one to three eggs after mating. The eggs are about 3 inches (7.6 centimeters) long. Young eagles hatch about six weeks later.

hatch
to break out of an egg

golden eagles

Eaglets

Young eagles are called eaglets. Light gray feathers called down cover an eaglet's body. After 10 to 13 weeks, the down turns to adult feathers. Parents bring eaglets food for about 12 weeks. Eaglets then learn to fly and hunt for their own food.

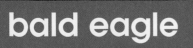
bald eagle

An Eagle's Nest

Eagles build nests called aeries (AIR-eez). Aeries are made of mud, twigs, bark, and leaves. They can be 6 to 20 feet (2 to 6 meters) deep. Some aeries weigh 6,000 pounds (2,700 kilograms). Most eagles build aeries at the top of tall trees. Other eagles build aeries on mountains.

twig
a small, thin tree branch

bald eagle

FUN FACTS

In 1782, the bald eagle became a national symbol of the United States.

Predators

Eagles have few predators. Raccoons and snakes sometimes steal eagle eggs for food. Humans sometimes harm eagles. People cut down trees where eagles build nests. People once killed eagles until they almost became extinct.

extinct
no longer living
anywhere in the world

African fish eagle

Eagles and People

People work to keep eagles from becoming extinct. Some people treat sick eagles and return them to the wild. People have passed laws against killing eagles. Laws also protect eagle habitats.

Hands On: Eagle Grip

Bald eagles grab fish from the water with their sharp talons. Bumps on eagles' feet help them hold onto the slippery fish.

What You Need

Handful of dirt or sand
Paper plate
Water
Bar of soap

What You Do

1. Spread the dirt or sand on the paper plate.
2. Wet your hands. Soap up your hands until they are full of suds.
3. Set the soap down. Place one hand on top of the dirt or sand. You should have a thin layer of dirt on your palm.
4. Pick up the bar of soap with the other soapy hand. Squeeze it and watch it slip out of your hand.
5. Now pick up the soap with the hand that has dirt or sand on it. Squeeze it and see if it slips out of your hand.

The hand with the dirt or sand on it grasped the bar of soap more tightly. The bumps on a bald eagle's foot work in much the same way. They help the eagle hold onto slippery fish.

Words to Know

down (DOUN)—the soft feathers of a young bird

extinct (ek-STINGKT)—no longer living anywhere in the world

habitat (HAB-uh-tat)—the place where an animal lives

mate (MATE)—to join together to produce young; male and female eagles mate to produce eaglets.

predator (PRED-uh-tur)—an animal that hunts and eats other animals

prey (PRAY)—an animal hunted by another animal; eagles are birds of prey; they hunt and kill prey to eat.

Read More

Kops, Deborah. *Eagles and Osprey.* Wild Birds of Prey. Woodbridge, Conn.: Blackbirch Press, 2000.

Martin-James, Kathleen. *Soaring Bald Eagles.* Pull Ahead Books. Minneapolis: Lerner, 2001.

Merrick, Patrick. *Eagles.* Nature Books. Chanhassen, Minn.: Child's World, 2000.

Internet Sites

All About Eagles
http://www.eagles.org/all.html
Bald Eagle
http://www.EnchantedLearning.com/subjects/birds/printouts/
 Eaglecoloring.shtml
Canadian Wildlife Service—Hinterland Who's Who—Bald Eagle
http://www.cws-scf.ec.gc.ca/cws-scf/hww-fap/bald/bald.html

Index